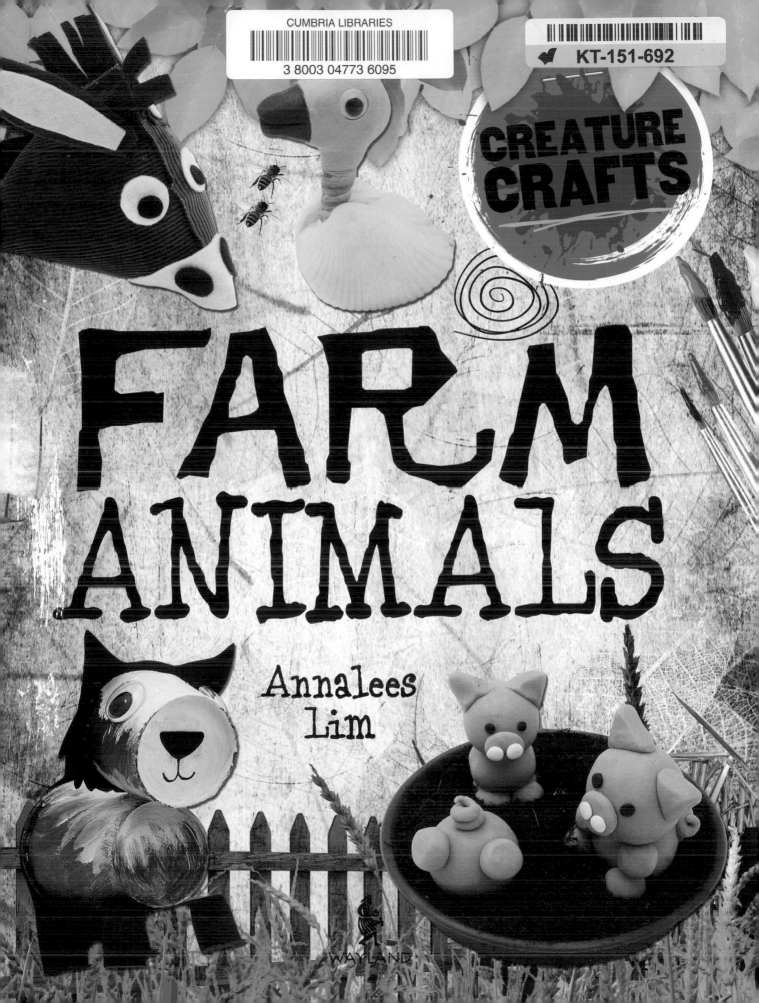

CREATURE CRAFTS

FARM ANIMALS

Annalees Lim

WAYLAND

CONTENTS

Welcome
to the world of
farm animals!

Do you know what kinds of animals live on a farm? Would you like to make some of those animals and find out loads of fun facts about them along the way? Then this book is for you!

Follow the easy step by step instructions to start creating your own farm animal collection. When you have finished making an animal, you can also think about the kind of shelter it might live in.

A lot of the projects use paint and PVA glue. Always cover surfaces with a piece of plastic or layers of old newspaper. Whenever you can, leave the project to dry before moving on to the next step. This avoids things getting stuck to each other or paint smudging.

So, do you have your craft tools at the ready? Then get set to make your crafty creatures and discover what makes each of them so special!

QUILLED CHICK

You will need:
Yellow, orange and black quilling paper or shredded paper
Glue stick
1 x A4 green card
1 x A4 yellow card

When chicks have just hatched, they have soft, yellow feathers and tiny wings. Make your own fluffy chick using quilled paper!

1

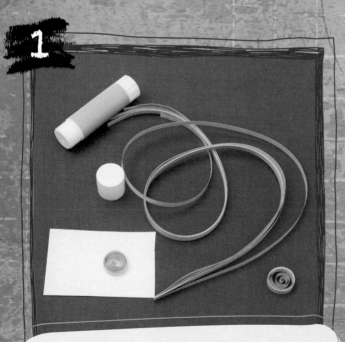

Take a yellow paper strip. Roll it into a loose coil and glue the end in place. Stick the coil onto yellow card. This is the head of the chick. Make a larger coil to form the body.

2

Make 2 smaller yellow coils. Pinch one end of each to create teardrop shapes. Stick them to the sides of the body to make the wings.

3

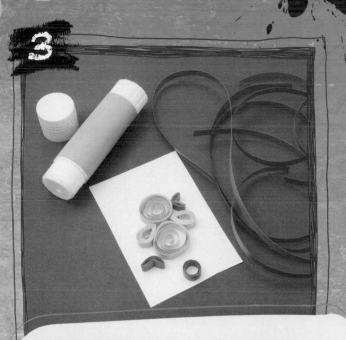

Make 3 small, orange coils. Flatten them and fold them into 'V' shapes. Stick two of them to the bottom of the body to make the feet, and one to the head to make the beak.

4

Make a small, tight black coil. Stick it into the head to make the eye. Cut around the chick.

5

Fold the green card to create a 'V' shape in the centre. Glue the quilled chick to the card.

CHICK FACT

Chicks are very small when they hatch. You could fit one inside your hand!

SHELL GOOSE

You will need:
Lots of shells
Orange paint
Paintbrush
White modelling clay
Scissors
Googly eyes

Geese like to live in groups, called gaggles. Use lots of shells of different sizes to make your unique gaggle of geese!

1

Roll a piece of modelling clay into a ball. Press a fan shell to each side to make the wings of your goose.

2

Press a long shell upright into the modelling clay in between the two shell wings. This will form the neck of your goose.

3

Roll a piece of modelling clay into a teardrop shape and press it onto the top of the shell neck. This will form the head of your goose.

4

Use scissors to cut into the narrow part of the head to form the beak.

5

Colour the beak using orange paint. Press googly eyes onto each side of your goose's head.

GOOSE FACT
Did you know that geese are water birds? They have webbed feet, which help them to swim across the water and walk on muddy ground.

WOOLLY HiGHLAND COW

You will need:
2 x A4 orange card
White card
1 x A4 green card
Orange wool
Glue stick
Scissors
Pencil
Sticky tape
Black marker pen

Highland cows are from Scotland, where the weather can get very cold. Make your Highland cow really woolly, so it stays warm!

1

Fold one piece of orange card in half. Draw a 'c' shape along the folded edge and cut out. This will form your cow's body and legs. Cut out 2 ears from the left-over orange card.

2

Fold the other piece of orange card in half and cut out a 'D' shape along the fold. Unfold the card and draw on your cow's nostrils.

3

Open out the legs and fold the bottom of each of them outwards. Stick the legs onto the green card. Cut 2 slits into your cow's head, one on each side of the fold.

4

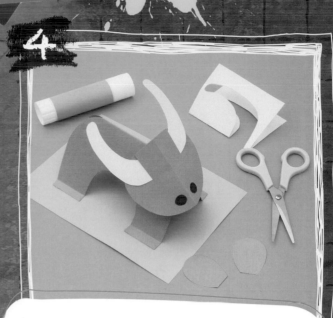

Fold white card in half and cut out a horn shape. Slide the unfolded horns through the slits. Use sticky tape to stick the cow's head onto its body. Glue both ears to its head.

5

Cut orange wool into short strips and glue those to the head and body of your cow.

HIGHLAND COW FACT
Highland cows are born without horns. They start growing them when they are 18 months old.

FLOCK OF SHEEP

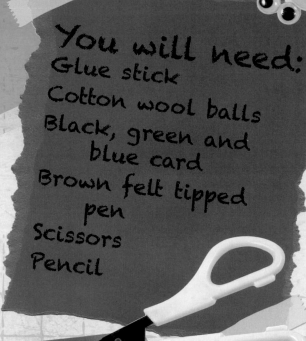

You will need:
Glue stick
Cotton wool balls
Black, green and blue card
Brown felt tipped pen
Scissors
Pencil

Sheep live in large groups, called flocks. Together, they graze on hillsides and in meadows. Make a large grassy hill for your own flock of sheep.

1

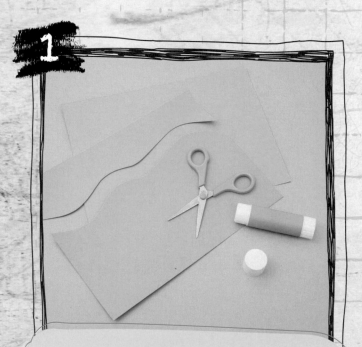

Cut some hill shapes out of the green card. Stick it on the blue card, using the glue stick.

2

Use the brown pen to draw fences on the hills.

Stick lots of cotton wool balls onto the hills using the glue stick.

Use a pencil to draw lots of sheep's heads and legs onto black card. Cut them out.

Glue the heads and legs onto the cotton wool balls.

SHEEP FACT
Did you know that we use sheep's wool to make clothes?

GOAT SOCK PUPPET

Goats are very clever animals. They can learn their name, and will come when you call them. You can teach this goat sock puppet even more tricks!

1

Cut the pipe cleaner in half. Then cut out 4 long triangles from black felt. They should be 1cm shorter than the pipe cleaners.

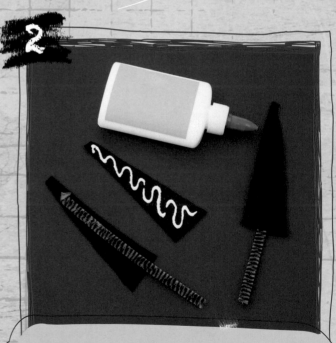

2

Glue a pipe cleaner between 2 felt triangles, leaving a bit of pipe cleaner sticking out at the bottom. Repeat, so that you have 2 sets. Leave to dry.

3

Cut out a circle of pink felt. It should be the size of the sole of the sock. Glue the pink circle to the sole to make the mouth of your goat.

4

Using the black, white, pink and brown felt, cut out your goat's ears, eyes, nose and a little beard. Stick them all onto the sock using fabric glue.

5

Twist the black felt triangles to make the horns. Stick the pipe cleaner ends into the sock and bend them to keep them in place.

GOAT FACT
Female goats are called nanny goats, male goats are called billy goats, and baby goats are called kids!

MUDDY PIGS

You will need:
Shallow flower pot
Soil
Pink, black & white modelling clay

Pigs bathe in mud to keep clean! The mud removes little bugs from their skin. You can make a muddy bath for your pigs, too!

1

Fill the flower pot with soil and press down firmly.

2

Use pink modelling clay to form a large ball, a medium-sized ball and 4 small balls. Also form 2 small triangles, a small squashed ball and a snake shape that you can curl up to form your pig's tail.

3

Press all the shapes together to form your pig. Make another set of shapes to form one sitting and one standing pig.

4

Use black modelling clay to form your pigs' eyes. Use white modelling clay to make your pigs' nostrils.

5

To make a pig that looks like it is digging into the soil, make a large ball, 2 small balls and a curly tail from pink modelling clay. Place all your pigs in the soil.

PIG FACT

Did you know that pigs are very clever? Some people say they are smarter than any other kind of farm animal or pet.

DUCK POND

Ducks spend most of their days swimming and diving in lakes and rivers. Make a pond with yellow ducklings that can swim and even dive!

You will need:
Zipped plastic pouch
Blue hair gel
Yellow & orange foam sheets
Scissors
Wide sticky tape
Craft glue
Dark green, light green & blue card
Googly eyes

1

Cut light green card and blue card to be as long as the plastic pouch. The light green card should be wider than the blue card. Cut a 'D' shape out of the light green card.

2

Cut 3 duckling shapes out of the yellow foam. Cut out beak shapes for the ducklings from the orange foam. Glue a beak and a googly eye to each duckling.

3

Stick the green card and the blue card from step *1* onto the pouch. Fill the bottom of the plastic pocket with blue hair gel.

4

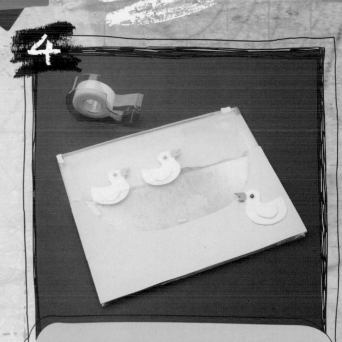

Place your ducklings inside the pouch, swimming on the hair gel. Seal the pouch with sticky tape.

5

Decorate the pond with blades of grass made from dark green card.

DUCK FACT
Did you know that ducks live in most parts of the world? You can find ducks on every continent on Earth, except Antarctica.

TRUSTY SHEEPDOG

Sheepdogs help out a lot on farms. They are very good at herding flocks of sheep. Why not train your sheepdog to herd all your farm animals?

1

Cut one of the paper cups to be half the height of the other one.

2

Paint both cups in black, grey and white, to look like fur.

3

Glue both cups on black card. Draw the outline of your dog's face around the small cup. Draw the outline of its back legs and tail around the big cup.

4

Cut out both shapes. Draw the ouline of your sheepdog's front legs on black card. Cut them out, too.

5

Glue the dog's head and front legs to its body. Cut out a nose from black card. Stick on the nose and googly eyes. Use a felt tipped pen to draw on a mouth.

SHEEPDOG FACT

Did you know that you can also keep sheepdogs as pets? They don't need to herd sheep, but they will need lots of exercise to stay happy.

DONKEY BEAN BAG

You will need:
Blue corduroy
Fabric glue
Rice
Black, pink, blue and white felt
Measuring tape
Scissors

Donkeys like living together in herds. They like living with goats, too. Your goat sock and your donkey could live together on your farm!

Cut out two squares of blue corduroy that are 15cm x 15cm.

Glue the squares one on top of the other, leaving one end open. Leave to dry completely before moving on to the next step.

3

Fill the bag with rice. Glue the top edges of the bag together in the opposite way to the bottom edges. This will make a triangular bean bag to form your donkey's head.

4

Cut out shapes from the felt to make a nose, ears, mane and eyes.

5

Glue all the shapes onto your donkey's head and leave to dry.

DONKEY FACT

A male donkey is called a Jack, and a female donkey is called a Jenny!

HORSE IN A STABLE

Horses are often used to herd cattle. Maybe your horse can herd your Highland cows! Keep your horse safe at night by making a stable for it to sleep in.

1

Measure the middle of the dark brown card. Fold each side into the middle. Make a firm crease along each fold.

2

Use the felt tipped pen to draw lines onto the front of the card flaps. These will make the stable doors for your horse.

3

Open up the stable doors. Use the felt tipped pen to draw the inside of the stable.

4

Draw the outline of a horse's head and neck onto the light brown card. Cut both out.

5

Cut both stable doors to create 2 small flaps at the bottom and 2 big flaps at the top. Stick your horse's neck to the stable wall. Fold over the bottom flaps and glue on its head. Stick on the googly eyes.

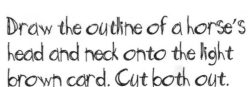

HORSE FACT
Did you know that horses can see behind them without turning their head?

GLOSSARY

continent	a big mass of land that is often made up of many countries
(to) hatch	when a chick breaks out of its egg
(to) herd	when an animal moves a group (or herd) of other animals
(to) remove	to take something away
unique	when something is one of a kind, not like anything else
webbed feet	feet where the toes are joined by pieces of skin

INDEX

Published in paperback in 2017 by Wayland
Copyright © Hodder and Stoughton 2017

Wayland, an imprint of Hachette Children's Group
Part of Hodder & Stoughton
Carmelite House, 50 Victoria Embankment,
London EC4Y 0DZ

All rights reserved.

Wayland, part of Hachette Children's Group and published
by Hodder and Stoughton Limited
www.hachette.co.uk

Series editor: Julia Adams
Craft photography: Simon Pask, N1 Studios
Additional images: Shutterstock

Dewey classification: 745.5-dc23
ISBN: 9780750297189
eBook ISBN: 9780750293761

10 9 8 7 6 5 4 3 2 1

Printed in China

FSC MIX Paper from responsible sources FSC® C104740